PROTECTION

Reference Notes

Originally published in 1956 as chapter 3 in
Infinite Way Letters 1955, by Joel Goldsmith.

Other Titles in This Series

PROTECTION

Joel S. Goldsmith

Acropolis Books, Publisher
Longboat Key, Florida

Protection by Joel S. Goldsmith

The Heart of Mysticism: The Infinite Way Letters 1955-1959
© 2007 by Acropolis Books

Acropolis Books, Inc.
Longboat Key, Florida
www.acropolisbooks.com

Except the Lord build the house,
they labour in vain that build it.

Psalm 127

Illumination dissolves all material ties and binds men together with the golden chains of spiritual understanding; it acknowledges only the leadership of the Christ; it has no ritual or rule but the divine, impersonal universal Love; no other worship than the inner Flame that is ever lit at the shrine of Spirit. This union is the free state of spiritual brotherhood. The only restraint is the discipline of Soul; therefore, we know liberty without license; we are a united universe without physical limits; a divine service to God without ceremony or creed. The illumined walk without fear – by Grace.

From the *The Infinite Way* by Joel S. Goldsmith

PROTECTION

IN THE MATERIAL SENSE of life, the word "protection" brings up the thought of defense or armor, a hiding place from an enemy, or some sense of withdrawal from danger. In the mental sciences, protection refers to some thought or idea, or some form of prayer that would save one from injury or hurt from an outside source. In the use of the word "protection" thought is immediately drawn to the fact that existing somewhere is a destructive or harmful activity or presence or power, and that protection, by word or thought, is a means of finding security from this danger to one's self or one's affairs.

In The Infinite Way we have learned that God is One: therefore, God is one power, and we live in that conscious One-ness. The moment the idea of God as One begins to dawn in consciousness we understand that in all this world there is no power and no presence from which we need protection. You will see this as you dwell on the word "Omnipresence," and realize that in this All-presence of Good you are completely alone with a divine harmony—a harmony which pervades and permeates consciousness, and is in itself the All-ness and the Only-ness of Good.

Ponder this idea and meditate upon it, and note how the revelation and assurance comes to you, within your own being, that this is true: there is but One, and because of the nature of that One there is no outside influence for either good or evil. There is no presence or power to which to pray for any good that does not already exist as Omnipresence, right where you are. In your periods of communion note the assurance that comes with the realization that God alone is, and that God's Presence is infinite. There is no other power; there is no other Presence; there is no destructive or harmful influence in any person, place or thing; there is no evil in any condition. God could not be One and yet find an existence separate and apart from that One. God alone is being— think of that, God alone is Being. How then can you pray to God in word or thought, or how can you defend yourself, mentally or physically, in the realization of God as being the One and the Only Being?

The Master has told us: "There is nothing from without a man, that entering into him can defile him: but the things which come out of him, those are they that defile the man."

3

Our studies and meditations have revealed that whatever of discord or inharmony is manifest in our experience today is coming through the activity of our own thought. We have accepted the universal belief of a power, a presence and an activity apart from God; we have accepted the belief that some one or some thing, outside of our own being, can be a presence or power for evil in our experience; and the acceptance of this rather universal belief causes much of our discord and inharmony.

As we consciously bring ourselves back, day after day, day after day, to the actual awareness of God as Infinite Being, God manifesting and expressing Itself as our individual being, we understand more fully that all power flows out from us, through us, as a benediction and blessing to the world, but that no power acts upon us from without our own being. As students of The Infinite Way, it must become clear to us that there is no power acting upon us from without our own being for either good or evil. Just as we have learned that the stars, the creations of God in the heavens, cannot act upon us in accord with astrological belief, so we have learned that conditions of weather, climate, infection, contagion, or accident likewise cannot act injuriously upon those who have come into some measure, at least, of the understanding of the nature of God and the nature of individual being. We are constantly being reminded to become more and more aware of the nature of God, the nature of prayer, and the nature of individual being, so that we will understand ourselves as the off-spring of God, of whom it is truly said, "Son, thou art ever with me, and all that I have is thine."

All of human existence is made up of the belief of two powers—the good and the evil. All religion in its beginning was nothing more nor less than an attempt to find something to deliver us from external conditions or powers of evil. Even today most religions deal with a concept of God as being some kind of great Power which, if we can only reach It, will protect and save us from these destructive influences which, it is claimed, exist outside our own being.

Think seriously on this subject of protection or protective work, because each day we are faced with suggestions of impending or threatened dangers. Always some person, some place, or some thing is being presented as a great danger or destructive power which we must fear, or from which we must seek a God to save us. Of course, if there were such dangers, and if there were such a God, the world would have discovered, long before this, some way to reach that God.

God's All-ness makes it utterly impossible for any destructive or evil influence or power to exist anywhere—in heaven, on earth, or in hell—so do not make the mistake of thinking of God as some great power which is able to save you from a destructive person or influence if only you can reach Him. Do not make the common mistake of thinking that The Infinite Way is just another method of finding God, or another manner of praying to bring God's influence into your experience in order to overcome discord, error, evil, sin and disease. No! Rather, understand that this Message is bringing the awareness of God as One; of God as infinite individual being; of God as All-Presence and All-Power.

The universal belief in two powers, good and evil, will continue to operate in our experience until we individually—remember this, you and I individually—reject the belief of two powers. In the tenth chapter of Luke, you will read that the Master sent the seventy disciples out, "two by two, into every city and place, whither he himself would come." When the seventy returned they rejoiced, saying, "Lord, even the devils are subject unto us through thy name." But the Master replied, "... rejoice not, that the spirits are subject unto you: but rather rejoice, because your names are written in heaven."

In this age we need a great deal of protective thought, but the nature of that thought must be the realization that God's All-ness precludes the possibility of there ever existing a source of evil in the world itself, or one able to operate in individual experience. Our protective work, or our prayers for protection, must consist of the realization that nothing exists anywhere, at any time in our experience of the past, present or future, that is of a destructive nature. Through our studies and meditations eventually we will come to that God-contact within us, wherein we receive the divine assurance: "Lo, I am with you alway." This will not come as a protection against evil powers or destructive forces, but as a continuous assurance of One Presence, One Power, One Being, One Life, One Law. It is in this awareness of One-ness that we find our peace.

It would be a wonderful thing if students would take this subject of protection into daily meditation for the next month or two, saying nothing about it to anyone. Do not discuss or mention it, but just keep it a secret subject within yourselves until you arrive at a place in consciousness where you actually can feel that God is One, and that the secret of protection lies not in seeking a God to save or secure you against some outside intrusion, but rather that safety, security and peace are entirely dependent on your remembrance and realization of the truth of God as One—Infinite One.

Do you not see that the world is seeking peace (just as it is seeking safety and security) outside of its own being? Whereas, no peace, no safety and no security will ever be found except in our individual realization of God as One—the Only Being, Presence and Power. We cannot tell the world about peace or safety or security, but we can find it for ourselves and thereby let the world see by our experience that we have found a Way higher than superstitious belief in some power of good that miraculously saves us from some power of evil. We cannot tell the world that there is no danger from outside sources,

10

influences or powers, but our realization of this truth can make the harmony and completeness and perfection of our lives so evident that others, one by one, will turn to seek that which we have found.

What have we found? Have we found a God to whom we can pray, and from whom we can receive special favors that others, less favored, cannot receive? Have we found a God to whom we can pray and receive healing or supply or protection? No! No! We have found no such thing: we have found God as One; we have found God as our very being. We have found God to be the Life—not a life subject to sin, disease or death, but the One and Only Life; we have found God to be eternal and immortal Life, our very individual life. We have found God to be the Law—not a law that can be used to offset laws of heredity, infection, contagion or disease, but the One

Infinite, Omnipresent Law—maintaining and sustaining the harmony and perfection of Its own creation at all times.

God is One, and beside Him there is no other. Because we know the nature of God as One, we know the nature of prayer as the realization of One-ness.

> "Look unto me and be ye saved, all the ends of the earth: for I am God, and there is none else."
>
> Isaiah 45:22

SPIRITUAL RELIANCE

SPIRITUAL HARMONY COMES quickly when we have given up the desire or search for physical, or outer harmony. This is the inner meaning of the Master's words: "Peace I leave with you, my peace I give unto you: not as the world giveth, give I unto you." Divine Grace comes in proportion as we turn from all sense of human peace, prosperity or health, and seek the realization of "My Peace," which includes the health or harmony of Spirit.

Paul tells us: "Be not deceived; God is not mocked: for whatsoever a man soweth, that shall he also reap. For he that soweth to his flesh shall of the flesh reap corruption; but he that soweth to the Spirit shall of the Spirit reap life everlasting." We must understand that in the first case we are being warned against a faith, confidence, reliance or dependence on the creature—that is, that which appears as effect. However, to "sow to the Spirit," by placing one's reliance and trust and hope in the Infinite Invisible is to reap the things of the Spirit, and in this way we honor the Creator rather than the creature. This is what the prophet Isaiah meant when he warned the Hebrews against their faith in "... the work of their own hands, that which their own fingers have made," and a deep principle is revealed in this warning.

At this point of our unfoldment it is necessary to realize that we have left behind the Law of Moses, and that we have stepped out into the Grace of Truth. Surely by now we know that good humans are not rewarded by God, nor are bad humans punished by God. Whatever of reward or punishment comes into human experience comes through our own belief in such. Too often students complain bitterly about the problems they experience while on their search for God, not realizing how fortunate they are to be in the midst of these problems while seeking the revelation and realization of God, because until one has been divested of every human or material aid one cannot know the experience of a complete reliance on the Infinite Invisible.

We are born into a world where first we learn to rely on parents, later on teachers, husbands or wives, and often we end up dependent upon our children. In between we become dependent upon medicines and dollars, so that at no time in the average person's experience does he ever learn that there is an Infinite Invisible which is far better able to supply his every need, and far more dependable than any one or any thing in the visible realm. For the human, content to go through life in this way, it is naturally pleasurable to find at hand those people and things upon which he can rely, but fortunate is he if he does not come to the end of his rope and find that humans and material resources have failed him.

However, those who have set themselves on the search for God will find their journey shortened by every experience of failure on the part of friends and relatives and things, because then comes the complete reliance on that which has heretofore never been experienced—the Infinite Invisible. And what spiritual treasures we can bring forth through the realization to be gained from: "My grace is sufficient for thee," and "Man shall not live by bread alone, but by every word that proceedeth out of the mouth of God."

AN IMPORTANT POINT IN SPIRITUAL PRACTICE

SPIRITUAL PRACTICE, WHICH embraces all phases of the healing work, is much more than declaring or knowing some truth after a discord has been brought to your attention. Spiritual practice is a constant, conscious realization of God as Omnipresence—of God as the Life, Law, Substance, continuity, activity, the very Soul and intelligence of all being.

Suppose at this very moment you were to receive a call asking for help, and you proceed to give a treatment, to pray, or to go into meditation or communion. If, consciously or unconsciously, you have accepted the discord, and expect and hope that harmony is going to be restored through your treatment or prayer your success will be very limited, and your failures will be more numerous than your successes.

"When a call comes announcing some form of discord it is necessary to remember consciously that this is not a discord or maladjustment which, through your effort or even through God, is to be corrected, but rather that this is a specific call to know that as God was in the beginning, so God is now, and God ever will be!

Unless you are living the spiritual life in such a manner as keeps you in the realization that the past and the future are one—here and now in the present—you will find yourself in distress if a call comes saying, "My friend has just been killed: please help me." You will be in a very embarrassing position indeed, because you will be expected either to raise the dead or to accept death as an actual happening, and merely give a treatment or meditation for the comfort of the bereft one. This situation must never come to you: you must never be in such a state of consciousness where anyone can announce that someone has been killed or has passed on, and then from that point expect to do something spiritual about it.

In living the true spiritual life you are not waiting for calls of discord and inharmony. You are living in such a state of consciousness that God alone is the reality, and your entire experience is one of dwelling in the realization of God ever governing, maintaining and sustaining Its own universe—from the beginning of time until the end of the world.

"Before Abraham was, I am. I am with you alway, even unto the end of the world." This brings that past and the future into the present: if I am with you since before Abraham, nothing could have occurred before that call except that which was a part of the demonstration of I am—the all-inclusive Love, Presence and Power of God. If I am with you until the end of the world, nothing can happen today, tomorrow or next week which is not a part of the all-embracing guidance, direction and protection of the divine principle of this universe.

In ordinary metaphysical practice, consciously or unconsciously you accept the fact that there are those in the world who are suffering from discord and inharmony, and that at any moment someone may telephone or come in person asking for help, and if you are not very, very careful you will be tempted to give it. Unless you are already living in the consciousness of God as the omnipresent Law and Being, the omnipresent Good, the omnipresent direction, guidance, intelligence, wisdom, substance and reality, you will automatically attempt, through spiritual means, to bring about adjustments, healings, harmonies and resurrections, all based on the fact that a sin or disease, accident or death have already occurred.

The Infinite Way is not a practice that begins with a call for help. The Infinite Way is a way of life in which, at all times, we live and move and have our being in the realization of God as Omnipresence, and in that consciousness, whenever an appearance or call of discord reaches us, we are enabled to smile in the true knowledge that no discord or inharmony has ever happened, therefore is not now in need of adjustment.

Here is one of the most important points to be achieved on the Spiritual Path. At one time I was taught that practitioners should consciously and specifically know the truth every day: that all who needed me would find me. It took only twenty-four hours to learn that this was a denial of the Christ. How could I, in one breath, say, "Those who need me will find me," and in the next, when they came to me, say, "God governs you; God is your life; You are perfect now"? Do you not see that it is up to us to know, before anyone comes to us, that perfection was the true state of their being, and that perfection is the true state of their being in the here and now? Do you really believe that we have anything to do with establishing or bringing about harmony? No! No! Our place in the Spiritual Path is not to be repairers of damage nor resurrectors of life, nor physicians nor protective influences—that is God's function! And not only now, but from the beginning it has been God's function to be the creative principle of this universe, and to be the maintaining and sustaining principle unto all time.

If you understand the nature of God you will understand that God is the creative principle of all existence; God is the law unto all creation; God is the substance, the reality and the continuity of all creation. Therefore, all creation is in and of God, subject to God's government and God's care. It is your function to know this truth. Ye shall know this truth, and this truth will make you free— free of accepting appearances and then trying to do something about them.

Do you see wherein the Message of The Infinite Way, and its practice, differs from the greater part of metaphysical teachings? Living the Infinite Way means living in the constant, conscious realization of God as Infinite, Omnipresent, Eternal Being. It means living always in the consciousness that before Abraham was, I am the divine principle, the protective, maintaining and sustaining influence unto this universe. It also means living in the constant, conscious realization of the truth that I am with you unto the end of the world, and just as nothing could happen to you yesterday, so nothing could happen to you today or tomorrow, except as a part of God's Grace.

We could live lives of constant miracles if only we would abide in the consciousness of this truth: "My grace is sufficient for thee." Thy Grace is sufficient for every need, but not Thy Grace that is coming tomorrow. Thy Grace, since before Abraham was, is my sufficiency; Thy Grace is my sufficiency unto the end of the world. Thy Grace of the past, present and future is at this very instant my sufficiency in all things. Every day there are temptations to believe that we or our families or students are in need of something in the nature of form (it may be food, housing, opportunity, education, employment, rest) but to all those things we can respond: "Man shall not live by bread alone, but by every word that proceedeth out of the mouth of God," because Thy Grace is man's sufficiency in every instance.

From these two scriptural passages you can build such a consciousness of the omnipresence of the Infinite Invisible that forever after you will learn to love and enjoy and appreciate everything in the world of form and everything that exists as effect, yet never have the feeling that you need or require anything. Since God's Grace is your sufficiency you do not live by effect alone, but by every Word of Truth that has been embodied in your consciousness, and by every passage of Truth that you have made your own.

Affirming truths and denying errors will not make your demonstration. You must learn to live by every word of truth, and make every Word of Truth a part of your consciousness so that it becomes flesh of your flesh, bone of your bone, until the past, present and future are all bound up in the conscious realization of God's Grace as your sufficiency. In other words, your consciousness of Truth is the source and substance and activity and law of your daily demonstration of Good.

To those who are accepting the Message of The Infinite Way as a way of life, I would like to sum this up by asking that you go back and bring your past into your present by spending some time during this next month consciously realizing that God's Grace was your sufficiency in what you call your past; and that since before Abraham was, God's government of this universe has been so perfect that nothing of a discordant or inharmonious nature can happen to you or to anyone else, today or tomorrow. And so, should you hear of a sin, a disease, an accident or a death, immediately realize that it could not have happened, since from the beginning of time God has been the only law and reality unto His universe. Then you will know the true meaning of spiritual healing. You will know what Christ-consciousness is; you will know what it means to live and move and have your being in God-consciousness, never accepting appearances, temptations, discords, sins, diseases or accidents as anything other than temptations to believe in time and space.

If you are able to see that the past must become the present so that you are able to cover it all with the term I am, I am with you, I am with you in the past, I am with you in the present, I am with you since before Abraham was, I am is the law unto you, has been the law unto you, you will be able to take the next step and bring the future right down to the present, so that "unto the end of the world" will be embraced in your consciousness the consciousness of the Omnipresence of I am. In this way your whole universe will be embraced in the time and space since before Abraham was, unto the end of the world—all of it brought down to the here and now of I am with you.

The only time is God's time—now. God's time has existed since before Abraham was, and will continue to exist until the end of the world. Because I am with you since before Abraham was and unto the end of the world, I am is the immediate present—now. God's Grace now is your sufficiency, and the sufficiency unto your family and friends and students—and unto all who can accept God's Grace.

PUNISHMENT

SOMETIMES SECRETS, SO DEEP and so profound, are revealed to us that we are shaken from head to foot, and when this happens we learn something not only new, but something that must make a drastic change in our lives. Such is the experience when we realize the nature of punishment and the reasons for punishment in our experience.

To understand that God neither rewards nor punishes is an important step in your spiritual development. If you have been at all impressed with this statement, you have pondered and meditated upon it, and somewhere along this line of inner reflection you have come to the realization that all of the religious theories which have been taught on the subject of punishment have been erroneous, and this itself should have made a startling change in your life. If you have the courage to continue your inner cogitation along this line, ultimately you will be led to the truth about punishment and the reason for punishment, and this will give you the opportunity to remold your life.

God is individual being, which means that God is the only Self, and there is no way for any hurt or evil to enter to defile the infinite purity of the Soul of God, nor anything at which evil can strike or attach itself. God is the Self of you, therefore God is the Self of me, and if I were in any way to hurt or offend you, to whom is my offence directed but to myself? This clarifies the Master's words: "Inasmuch as ye have done it unto one of the least of these my brethren, ye have done it unto me:" and with this understanding you begin to see that every bit of good done by you at any time in your entire life has been a good done to, for, and within yourself; and you also begin to see that every evil or thought of evil you have ever directed toward another, every lie and evasion of truth has been directed toward your own self, and therefore the punishment is inflicted upon you by you, because your act or thought of deceit, supposedly directed toward another, was actually directed toward yourself.

When the Master repeated the age-old wisdom: "Wherefore all things whatsoever ye would that men should do to you, do ye even so to them: for this is the law and the prophets;" He was giving us a principle: unless we do unto others as we would have others do unto us, we injure not the others but ourselves. In this present state of human consciousness it is true that the evil thoughts and dishonest acts and thoughtless words that we send out to others do harm them temporarily, but in the end always it will be found that the injury was not nearly so much to them as it was to ourselves.

In the days to come, when men recognize the great truth that God is the Selfhood of each individual, the evil aimed at us from another will never touch us, but will immediately rebound upon the one who sends it. In the degree that we recognize God as our individual being, we also realize that no weapon that is formed against us can prosper, since the only "I", the only "Me", is God, and we will not fear what man can do to us, since the Selfhood of us is God and cannot be harmed, and our realization of this will quickly send back the evil, and much more quickly than has heretofore been the case.

Once the first realization of this truth comes to us we understand that there is no longer any use concerning ourselves with what our neighbor does unto us, but looming large in our consciousness will be the realization that we must watch ourselves—morning, noon and night we must watch our thoughts, our words, our actions, to see that we ourselves do not send out anything of a negative nature which would be bound to have its result within our own being.

Never for a moment believe that this will result in your being good in order to avoid punishment. This revelation goes far deeper than that: it enables you to see that God is your Selfhood, and that anything of an erroneous or negative nature that emanates from any individual is given power only in the degree that you yourself give it power. In your meditation it will result in the revelation of the nature of your true being—of God as the nature of your Life and Soul, and in that realization you will see that this is the truth of all men, and that the only way and mode of successful living is to understand your neighbor to be yourself.

And so it is that whatever of good or of evil you do unto others, you do unto the Christ of your own being—"Inasmuch as ye have done it unto one of the least of these my brethren, ye have done it unto me."

WHY?

WHEN HELP IS ASKED on certain physical or mental conditions, the question is often asked: Why is the so-called spiritual healing only a partial healing, and why sometimes is it never a complete healing? Also, why is it that a person about to undergo surgery asks for help and receives a miraculous healing, although not one that precludes the necessity for surgery? Why is it that the patient undergoing surgery is kept entirely free of infection or after-effect and makes a more rapid recovery than would normally be the case, and yet, if God has anything to do with that much of the healing, why did not God make the surgery unnecessary?

First of all, you must understand that there are no degrees of Truth. Truth is absolute. God is absolute. God is absolute Truth; God is absolute Being; God is infinite, eternal, immortal, omnipresent perfection. God is all. Therefore, the all-ness in the infinity and completeness and perfection of God being established, any measure less than that, experienced by the patient, represents the conditioned state of consciousness which makes it impossible to bring through or realize the completeness of the activity of God.

Here you have two factors: the consciousness of the practitioner and the consciousness of the patient. Let us assume that the consciousness of the practitioner is far higher and deeper than that of the patient, and so the patient comes to the practitioner with a conditioned state of consciousness in which it is not possible for him to open his consciousness completely to the fullness of the activity of God. It may be that there is so much attachment to the body and to the sense of personal health that the patient does not completely let go, and thus receive the full benefit of the infinite completeness and perfection of the activity of God as individual consciousness. Although the practitioner may be an instrument for a complete and perfect healing, the conditioned consciousness of the patient does not always allow this to come through.

On the other hand, the practitioner may not be up to the experience of the miracle of complete healing. To be in the highest state of consciousness, the practitioner has reached that elevation of spiritual awareness in which no effort is ever made to contact God for the purpose of healing. He is abiding in the consciousness of God as individual being, hence in the realization that the individual is already at the standpoint of immortality and eternality, that state of being to which nothing can be added.

The practitioner who is trying to use Truth over error, who is contacting God for the purpose of establishing harmony, or who is still in the third dimension of life, in which body is something separate and apart from spiritual consciousness, will make the mistake of being concerned with health as against disease, or will permit himself to be concerned with what appears to be something less than perfection in the visible scene.

For perfect healing the practitioner must abide in the consciousness of God as the infinite all, which means abiding in the fourth dimension of life in which no recognition is given to the pairs of opposites—good and evil, rich and poor, moral and immoral, immortal and mortal. In this fourth dimensional consciousness, or Christ-consciousness, the practitioner is never aware of someone or something to be healed or corrected, but is always aware of the Omnipresence of God's Being.

When the practitioner is able to abide in Christ-consciousness and have always "that mind which was also in Christ Jesus", then the fullness of God's Being freely flows, and regardless of whether it is an acute illness or a chronic one, or whether the illness is at the point of surgery, the practitioner can bring to conscious realization and demonstration the complete healing or unfoldment of divine harmony. When the practitioner's consciousness is at all conditioned, then the healing can only come through in proportion to the degree of conditioning of the practitioner's consciousness. In order to complete the experience of instantaneous or complete healing, the patient also must approach this work without the conditioned thought of believing that the power of God can bring one through illness, even though not able to perform the entire unfoldment of harmony without the aid of surgery. At least, the patient should be able to relax with no preconceived thought or opinion as to what will take place, and let the divine consciousness of the practitioner have full sway.

You can readily see that the main responsibility rests with the practitioner. When the practitioner truly rises above the pairs of opposites to that state of consciousness in which all sense of both health and disease are absent, and when any phase of the human picture does not bring a reaction which has behind it the desire to heal, correct, save, renew or regenerate, then in that spiritually illumined state of consciousness the practitioner will bring through greater works.

As you approach that state of non-reaction to the world of appearances whereby you do not react happily to the good appearances, and certainly do not react fearfully or doubtfully to the evil appearances, you will do far greater healing works, and will be able to impart to those who come to you a greater confidence in the great Truth that God is, which means that harmony is, perfection is, reality is—and, in spite of all appearances to the contrary, good alone is.

Printed in Great Britain
by Amazon